THE WORDS OF THE BIBLE

7

PSALMS
OF
MERCY

St Paul Publications
The Liturgical Press

PSALMS OF MERCY

Original title: *I salmi della misericordia*
© 1989 Figlie di San Paolo, Milan, Italy
English language edition first published in February, 1993

Translated by Luigi Bertocchi OSB

Australian edition:
© St Paul Publications, 60-70 Broughton Rd (PO Box 230),
Homebush NSW 2140
National Library of Australia
Card Number and ISBN 1 875570 17 9

North American edition:
© The Order of St Benedict, Inc.,
The Liturgical Press, Collegeville, Minnesota 56321
ISBN 0-8146-2162-7

Typeset by St Paul Publications, Homebush, Australia
Printed by Singapore National Printers, Singapore

CONTENTS

FOREWORD

The psalms, which report prophecy, are the prayer of God's people yesterday, today and tomorrow. They let us penetrate God's mystery and help us to feel God's goodness, affection, and mercy for everybody.

If we pray the psalms constantly, it becomes easier to instil God's love into our daily lives.

This collection of twenty psalms contains a particular expression of God's mercy.

When we sin, the easiest way to find peace is to fix our attention and all our being onto the immensity of God's love, allowing Jesus, God's tenderness, to envelop and fill our lives.

With such an inner experience then, the child becomes an adult, the sick recover, the distressed find joy again, the frail become strong, the sinner acquires love.

Human life, lived in God's mercy, radiates a song of praise, peace and joy.

After each complete or partial psalm comes a short meditation placed in the evangelical context. Quotations help enrich the message of the psalm.

The Publishers

MY GOD LIKES UTOPIA TOO

How terrible it would be if it were otherwise.

God is my saviour, the reason of my life. God is not just a grain of sand but an ocean of greatness, an horizon that embraces, a sun that charms.

This is the God in whom I would like to put all my dreams, my sorrows, my sins, my continual waiting and seeking...

I know that God is mercy, liberation, fullness. I know that God has broken my chains of evil, swept away the obstacles and defences of my sin. God has overcome weakness and death. Therefore why lower my eyes and sit weeping? If my eyes weep, they will not do so for long. God is close. God's presence and tenderness comfort me. God has forgiven my sin, healed my wounds. God has made me a child and an heir.

To pray the psalms means to meet God, imploring the divine goodness, through which I may overcome rapidly the vicissitudes of life that prevent me from looking ahead and contemplating the shining horizon.

I feel emotions of pure faith, alternated with sadness, when I discover that I do not live as son or daughter, sister or brother of Jesus in my everyday life.

Do not despair! Everything will be embraced by God in Jesus Christ. In every type of difficulty, God is present.

Giorgio De Capitani

GIVE THANKS TO GOD WHO IS GOOD; WHOSE MERCY ENDURES FOR EVER

GOD SUPPORTS US IN DIFFICULT TIMES

from Psalm 27

O God, listen when I call,
pity me and answer me.
My heart tells me to seek your face;
your face, O God, will I seek.
Do not turn away from me,
nor in your anger dismiss your servant;
you have always been my help.

Never leave me, never desert me,
O God, my saviour.
Though my father and mother forsake me,
God will receive me.
O God, teach me your way;
lead me by a level path.

I still believe firmly
that I shall see God's goodness
in the land of the living.
Wait for God;
be strong and take heart
and wait for God.

The presence of the evil which is spreading in the world and which snares each of us, runs up against an insurmountable wall: God's grace and mercy (cf. 2 Cor 12:9), which become a warm voice and a friendly presence (cf. Jn 6:20). This grace and mercy give us the strength to give ourselves to God, like Jesus (cf. Lk 23:46). Only the person who confides in God's mercy (cf. Eph 2:4-5), and seeks God, can regain hope, peace, and tranquillity along the path of life.

God
Evil, as driving rain,
haunts my hope
in your infinite love.
But my heart cannot be afraid.
I ask you, O God,
for the sweetness
of your home.
I seek your face
on this desert land,
where you have rescued me.

GOD SETS US FREE
AND SAVES US

from Psalm 30

O God, I will exalt you,
for you have raised me up,
and have not let my foes gloat over me.
O God, my God,
I called to you for help,
and you healed me.
O God, you brought me back from the grave,
you saved my life as I sank into the pit.

We sing to you, we your faithful ones,
we praise your holy name.
Your anger passes in a moment,
but your favour lasts a lifetime;
weeping may last through the night,
but cries of joy come with the dawn.

When I was wealthy I used to think,
'I can never be shaken!'
O God, when you favoured me,
you made me as firm as a mountain;
and when you hid your face from me,
I was dismayed.

I called to you, O God;
I cried to you for mercy:
'What do you gain from my death,
by my falling into the pit?
Will the dust give praise to you?
will it proclaim your faithfulness?'

Jesus has introduced us to the secrets of God's mercy. This mercy awaits the person who has gone away (cf. Lk 15:11 ff.), finds the on who has lost the way (cf. Jn 4), lifi the one who has fallen (cf. Lk 18:8-9); — saves and brings all to a new life in Christ (cf. Eph 2:4-5). God's infinite love embraces the matter with which we have been made and satisfies us with mercy and forgiveness. In this way, God's plan of love is completed.

My thanks...
to you, O God,
sincere, like my love
for your holy name.
Although various instincts
sadden my spirit,
your kindness is for ever.
In the evening,
weariness and regret.
But at dawn,
some light
is enough to give me hope.

GOD OUR PROTECTOR

from Psalm 121

I lift up my eyes to the hills;
where will my help come from?
My help comes from you, O God,
who made heaven and earth.
You will not allow my foot to slip;
my guardian will not slumber.

Guardian of Israel,
you neither slumber nor sleep.
You watch over me,
the shade on my right;
the sun will not harm me by day,
nor the moon by night.
You will keep me from all harm,
you will guard my life;
You will guard my coming and going,
both now and for eternity.

*F*or our life's journey, Jesus has given us the assurance of having a God who takes care of each of us (cf. Mt 6:32), loves each of us (cf. 1 Jn 4:10), dwells with those who love God (cf. Jn 14:23), and watches over those in the chosen flock (cf. Lk 12:32). God's tenderness enfolds the universe. Everything becomes peaceful and secure in the sweet and vigilant hand of God — the guardian and the companion of each and every person.

Is my church...
in a valley
or on a mountain top?
It is all the universe,
and every path
is its!
To walk that path
we need a warm
and faithful hand.
Yours
O God!

SHOW ME THE WAY
I SHOULD GO

from Psalm 143

O God, hear my prayer;
listen to my supplications.
By your constancy and justice,
answer me.
Do not bring your servant to trial,
for no one alive is guiltless to you.

I stretch out my hands to you;
I thirst for you like an arid land.
O God, answer me quickly;
my spirit faints with worry.

Do not turn your face from me,
or I will be like those cast into the pit.
At dawn bring me word of your faithful love,
for I have put my trust in you;
show me the way I must go,
for I lift up my soul to you.
O God, save me from my foes,
for I find protection in you.

Teach me to do your will,
for you are my God;
may your gracious spirit guide me
on to level ground.
For the sake of your name
save my life, O God;
in your justice,
save me from trouble.

Every day we experience our fragile nature. But we also experience the resurrection: when we present ourselves to God with humility (cf. Lk 18:13), when our lack of trust becomes a petition to God (cf. Mk 9:24), when life is seeking God's face (cf. Jn 14:8). The openness to God, the obedience to God's will, the consciousness of the need of being forgiven and enlightened about our 'path' are necessary in order that our daily life be in harmony with the Spirit (cf. Rom 8:4).

I know I am a reed
But I do not bend when the wind blows.
I prefer to be broken.
My conscience is everything for me.
Better to be smashed to smithereens
than to flatter every trend.
The land is dry,
my lips are thirsty,
some pure water
is like a longing for freedom.

ETERNAL MERCY

from Psalm 118

We give thanks to you, for you are good,
your faithful love is eternal.
Let the house of Israel say,
your faithful love is eternal.
Let the house of Aaron say,
your faithful love is eternal.
Let those who fear God say,
your faithful love is eternal.

When I called in distress to you,
you heard me and set me free.
You are with me, I shall not fear;
what can anyone do to me?

With you with me as my help,
I gloat over all my enemies.

My strength and my song is you,
you have become my salvation.
Shouts of joy and salvation
fill the tents of the just:
'O God, your right hand has done wonders!
Your right hand is lifted high
Your right hand has done wonders!'

I will not die, but live
and proclaim what you have done.

*F*east, *praise, joy to the infinite mercy which performs wonders: creates (cf. Ps 103), gives life (cf. Jn 1:4), renews (cf. Rev 21:1), has become visible in Christ, an individual temple (cf. Jn 2:21) of God's glory, who has made each person's face God's temple (cf. 1 Cor 6:19).*

God is good...
and loves us always.
These rocks,
these deserts,
these oceans
are God's witness.
And my heart
sees God
as the heart
of humanity
since the beginning of time.
For every person
who enters your temple,
the first cry
is in praise of life
to you,
infinite and humble God,
since you are in me.

HAVE MERCY ON ME, O GOD, IN YOUR FAITHFUL LOVE

FROM SIN TO NEW LIFE

from Psalm 51

Have mercy on me, O God, in your faithful love;
in your great compassion
blot out my offences.
Wash away all my misdeeds,
and cleanse me from my sin.
For I know my transgressions,
and my sin is always in mind.

I have sinned against you, only you,
and done what you see to be wrong;
you are justified in your sentence
and blameless in your judgment.

I have surely sinned from birth,
a sinner from my conception,
but you want truth in the inner being,
so put your wisdom into my secret heart.

Cleanse me with hyssop until I am clean;
wash me, that I may be whiter than snow.
Let me hear joy and gladness,
let the bones you have broken rejoice.
Turn your face from my sins,
and blot out all my misdeeds.
Create a pure heart in me, O God;
renew a resolute spirit within me.

Do not thrust me from your presence;
do not remove your spirit of holiness.
Give me back the joy of salvation;
sustain me with a willing spirit.

When our life is torn into pieces because of sin (cf. Mt 27:4), when our tears are not enough to cleanse our faults (cf. Mt 14:72), look at Jesus, 'whom they pierced' (cf. Jn 19:37), and meet the one who is the victim of expiation for our sins, who pleads for each of us (cf. 1 Jn 2:1-21).

Even my sinning...
is in front
of your eyes;
yet, you look upon me
with love,
as I look back at you.
How could I live
and not beg
mercy?
Give me back
the joy of being saved.
Thus I shall rise to new life
and I will be able to show
your eternal love
to those who do not know you.

PATHS OF LIFE

from Psalm 25

To you, O God,
I lift up my soul.
I put my trust in you, my God;
do not let me be put to shame,
nor let my foes exult over me.

None who hope in you
will ever be put to shame;
let them be shamed
who break faith without cause.
Make your ways known to me, O God,
and teach me your paths;
Lead me in your truth and teach me,
for you are my God, my saviour,
and I wait for you all the day long.

O God, remember your faithful love and mercy,
for they have been yours forever.
Do not remember the sins of my youth
and my transgressions;
but remember me in your faithful love,
and in your goodness, O God.

O God, you are good and just;
you teach sinners to go your way.
You lead the humble in what is right,
and teach them your way.

For the sake of your name, O God,
forgive my sin, however great.

The Son of God came to redeem sinners (cf. Mk 2:17), and he scandalised the people. He invited them to his stable (cf. Lk 2:8 ff.). He wanted them to dine with him (cf. Mt 9:10). He helped them by his miracles (cf. Lk 5:20). He called them by name (cf. Lk 19:5). He wanted them beside his cross (cf. Mt 27:38). He took them to paradise (cf. Lk 23:43). He gave them the message of the resurrection (cf. Jn 20:17). Again and again, he put them on new paths, the paths of, and to life.

You are mercy
You never forget that.
The more we are sinners
the longer you remember your promises.
My past sins are gone and today
my petition is for a new path.
Free my foot from the snare of evil,
and from my feeling useless,
alone, unhappy.
I trust in you, O God of salvation.

PEACE OF FORGIVENESS

from Psalm 32

Blessed are those whose faults are forgiven.
whose sins are covered;
they are blessed whom God says are guiltless,
whose spirit harbours no deceit.

While I kept silent, my body was wasting
because of my groaning
all the day long,
for day and night your hand lay heavy,
and sapped my strength like summer heat.
Then I admitted my sin to you
and I did not hide my iniquity.
I said, 'I will tell all my faults to God',
and you forgave my sinful guilt.

Let all who are faithful turn to you
while you may be found;
when the mighty waters rise
they will never reach them.
You are a place where I can hide,
you will save me from trouble
and surround me with salvation.

I will teach you and show you
the way you should go;
I will advise you
and watch over you.

*The ups and downs of life,
enthusiasms, and depressions,
alternate to torment, to carry away,
to dishearten, and to make joyful
the human creature, who everyday
experiences sin. At the same time,
this human creature experiences the
desire for God and the need for
forgiveness. The hard exhausting
struggle against evil (cf. Lk 11:24-26),
which engages all of us (cf. Rom
7:19), finds a solution and the
creature can relax by plunging into
God's mercy (cf. Jn 3:8), like
children into their father's arms. To
recognise our own poverty and to
confess it to God (cf. Jn 1:8-9), is to
be in a state of blessedness and
peace.*

You know very well. . .
my heart, O Lord.
My struggle is not unfamiliar to you,
and my groaning because of evil.
You keep your eyes on me,
on the wide waters of this immense sea.

THE NAME THAT SAVES

from Psalm 79

O God, the nations have invaded your heritage,
defiled your temple,
laid waste to Jerusalem;
do not count our ancestors' sins
against us;
let your mercy
come quickly to meet us,
for we are in desperate need.

O God, our saviour, help us
for the glory of your name;
deliver us, forgive our sins,
for the sake of your name.
Why should the nations ask,
'Where is their God?'

Let us see your servants' blood
avenged among the nations.
Let the prisoners' groans
rise before you;
by your arm's strength,
save the condemned.

Then we, your people,
the sheep of your pasture,
will praise you forever;
from age to age
we will tell your praise.

In place of an outward and empty piety, Jesus has set the inwardness of our relationship with God (cf. Mt 6:1-17), lived under the influence of the Spirit (cf. Jn 4:23-24), centred on the only name that gives salvation (cf. Acts 4:12). The mystery of love, mercy, forgiveness, and purification is Jesus who shed his blood for us (cf. Heb 9:12-14), who offers himself to God as an ever-living petition in order that our sin cannot be set down against us (cf. 2 Cor 5:19). He has conquered and destroyed it for us.

We are skillful builders...
of churches, O God.
But we incense your name
without the fragrance of spirit and truth.
We are your temple, but our worship
is from a physical heart,
not a spiritual one.
And the nations laugh at us, and at you
because of our prayers
mumbled in churches, ruins of a faith,
devoid of respect for the person.

THE ROAD OF FREEDOM

from Psalm 102

You will arise to show Zion mercy,
for it is time to pity it;
the appointed time has come.
Its stones are dear to your servants;
its very dust moves them to pity.
The nations will fear your name, God,
and all the rulers of the earth your glory.

For you will rebuild Zion
and appear in your glory.
You will hear the plea of the destitute,
and will not scorn their prayer.
Let this be recorded for a future generation,
for a people not yet born to praise you, God.

O God, you leaned down from the heights of
your sanctuary,
you have looked down from heaven to earth,
to hear the groans of the prisoners
and release those under sentence of death,
to proclaim your name in Zion
and your praise in Jerusalem;
when nations and realms
will gather together, to worship you.

God does not regret love: to the creature's cry of rebellion, God answers with the cry of mercy. In Jesus made flesh, God restores us, and makes us free creatures again, able to love. When personal and social self-sufficiency (cf. Mt 7:21) make us slaves of sin and suffocate life (cf. Jn 8:34), just at the right moment the proposal of the Lord (cf. Mt 16:24) shows us the pathway of freedom (cf. Jn 8:31).

Even my home too...
suffers neurosis
because of limited horizons;
and to live there
is to be a fading shadow.
The time has come, O God,
to rebuild
a new world
where freedom and conscience
will become
laws of life.

YOU, MY GOD,
ARE
MY MERCY

EVERYTHING IS JOY

from Psalm 68

We sing to you, God, sing praise to your name,
extol you who ride on the clouds;
rejoice in you and dance before you.
Guardian of orphans, the widows' defender,
such are you in your holy dwelling.

You give a home to the friendless,
you lead the prisoner to safety.
O God, when you marched at the head of your
people,
when you strode through the desert places,
the earth shook and the heavens poured rain
at the presence of God,
the God of Israel.

O God, you rained a shower of blessings;
your weary inheritance
was filled with strength.
Your people settled, and in your goodness,
O God, you provided for the poor.

Blessed be God who daily carries burdens for us,
God our saviour.
Our God is a God who saves us;
from our God comes escape from death.

*L*ife and history are filled with the wonders of God (cf. Lk 1:67-79). God remembers the alliance with us, visits us, redeems and saves us. God directs our steps towards peace (cf. Lk 1:68-79). In this way today becomes a moment of salvation (cf. Lk 1:46-55). This moment expresses itself with benediction and praise (cf. Eph 1:3-14).

Years already passed...
and not forgotten
speak of you to us,
O God of mercy.
And today
is full of infinite graces,
sometimes lost
in the midst of sand castles.
Our ups and downs
are life
which comes from you,
the eternal living One.
They are life which goes
towards an horizon
of light.

SERENITY

from Psalm 131

O God, my heart is not proud,
my eyes are not raised too high;
I do not take part in great affairs,
in marvels beyond my capacity;
I keep myself in calm and quietness,
my soul within me is like a weaned child.
Israel, hope in God,
now and for eternity.

To grow, to exceed every limit is an innate yearning in all of us (cf. Sir 17:1-12), and there is a manner of satisfying this yearning in God's way (cf. Mt 18:3-4), enabling us to have rest in God (cf. Lk 10:21), causing our joy to burst forth (cf Lk 1:52). Trusting in God, with the same feelings of confidence, humility, and disposability as Mary, it is certain we will acquire peace and serenity.

O my God...
I am looking for freedom,
and I do not know
if to seek
is pride.
I feel serene,
like a child
in it mother's
arms.

UNBOUNDED CONFIDENCE

from Psalm 3

You are the shield at my side, O God;
my glory, you hold my head up high.
Whenever I cry to you,
you answer me from your holy hill.
I lie down to sleep,
and I wake up again,
for you uphold me.

I do not fear forces in thousands and thousands
drawn up against me on every side.
Arise, O God, save me, my God!
You strike all my foes against the face;
you break the teeth of the wicked ones.
From you, O God, comes deliverance.
May you bless your people.

This psalm is ruled by the mystery of Christ whose passion continues in the church, which, in turn, must repeat and live the mystery of its saviour. During his daily persecution (cf. Mt 9:19), in constant deadly danger (cf. Jn 8:29), Jesus had faith (cf. Jn 8:40) that he would not be abandoned when everything seemed to be over (cf. Lk 23:46).

Sunbeam
Already at dawn
I invoke you, O God.
Give peace
to your people,
in pain
because of the continual oppression
of violence
and sadness.
This first
sunbeam
opens my heart.

SAVING MERCY

from Psalm 9

I praise you, O God, with all my heart,
and tell of all your wonderful deeds.
O Most High, I rejoice and delight in you,
and sing to your name.

God, you reign forever,
you have set up your throne for judgment.
You will judge the world in justice,
and govern the people with fairness.
You are safety for the oppressed,
a fortress in troubled times.

Those who know you by name will trust in you;
O God, you never desert those who seek you.

Jesus has sent a warm invitation to the oppressed, always present in our world: 'Come to me ... and I will give you rest' (Mt 11:28), and he has given them the secret for living (cf. Mt 5:1-12) as he directs attention onto God and gives relief (cf. 1 Pet 5:7). In this way, sentiments of deep gratitude arise in the 'poor of the Lord'. These feelings impel them to manifest their joy in a song of praise to the Lord Jesus, the mercy which saves (cf. Jn 3:17-18).

Thanks, O God
God of infinite kindness,
my enemies are bending their knees.
I too, sometimes, in front of them.
And you, O God, raise me up with gentleness.
The poor are never forgotten
although still poor.
And they forget you because they are injured
by the hypocritical goodness of the people
who mock your kindness, O God.
You perceive, O God, my pain
and the suffering of the repressed.
You observe everything and take it within
your hands.

PRAISE TO GOD'S MERCY

from Psalm 135

We praise your name, O God,
Your servants praise you,
they who serve in the house of God,
in the courts of the house of our God.
They praise you, God, for you are good;
they sing to your name, your gracious name.
For you chose Jacob to be your own,
and Israel to be your prized possession.

I know that you are great, O God,
that you are greater than all the gods.
You do whatever you will,
in the heavens and on the earth,
in the seas to the furthest depths.

You form clouds from the ends of the earth;
the lightning splits them and it rains;
you bring the winds from your stores.
O God, your name will last forever,
your fame, O God, throughout the ages.

Our God is love and providence for all people. Gratitude and praise should sprout spontaneously and unceasingly. Everyone can understand the infinite reasons for that gratitude and praise. In the life of each of us, there are traces of God (cf. Acts 17:26-28). They are the reasons for constant praise (cf. Eph 5:19), the reflection of the experience of the Virgin Mary (cf. Lk 1:46), forerunner of the eternal song (cf. Rev 7:10-12).

The love you lavish on us
From this rustic corner
of honest people
I see you, O God,
and I praise
your becoming silent peace,
and shouting of children,
the rustling of leaves;
and I consider
the love you have for us,
although the noise of the crowd
makes your voice less audible.
I love you, I see you, I sense you.

TURN TO ME
IN
YOUR INFINITE MERCY

GOD HEARS THE HUMBLE

from Psalm 34

Come, my children, listen to me;
I will teach you to reverence the Most High.
If you relish your life,
and would like many days
with time to enjoy prosperity,
guard your tongue from evil,
and your lips from deceit;
turn from evil and do good;
look for peace and pursue it.

God's eyes are on the just,
God's ear is turned to their cry;
God turns away from evil,
to blot the memory of them from the earth.
They cry out in anguish and the Most High
hears;
and rescues them from all their troubles.

God is close to the broken hearted
and saves those whose spirit is crushed.
The just may have many troubles,
but God saves them from them all.
God guards every bone of the body;
not one of them will be broken.

But evil brings death to the wicked,
the foes of the just will be condemned.
O God, you ransom the lives of your servants;
none who take refuge in you are condemned.

The victims of evil done by others (cf. Lk 16:20-21), or the poor tried by sorrow (cf. Lk 7:13), let them meet the penetrating glance of Jesus (cf. Lk 18:38) and become witnesses of the presence and tenderness of God (cf. Mk 5:20). God, indeed, shares the secrets of life with people who have pure hearts and guileless looks (cf. Mt 11:25-26). God lets us discover the signs of the kindness that God put into the heart of every person.

You are always present
Why don't you seek God?
God will answer.
Look at your God,
and your face will rejoice.
God listens to the cry of the poor
while the rich shall have to beg.
The good thing is to look for peace;
anywhere you are peace will reach you.
God is close
to the one who has a wounded heart.
You, O God, are good.
You are always present

MERCY — OUR REFUGE

from Psalm 36

Sin speaks to the wicked
deep within their hearts;
there is no fear of God
before their eyes.
They so flatter themselves
in their own sight
that their sin and hatred
cannot be exposed.

The words of their mouths
express lies and malice;
they have ceased to be wise
and do good.
Even in bed they plot evil
and settle upon a sinful plan;
there is no wickedness
too great for them.

Your faithful love, O God,
reaches to the heavens;
your faithfulness reaches to the skies.
Your justice is like a mountain range;
your judgments are like the mighty deep.

You are a fountain of life;
your light gives us light.
Maintain your faithful love
to those who know you;
sustain your justice
to those whose heart is honest.

To the people entangled in the problems caused by remoteness from God (cf. 1 Cor 6:9), Jesus repeats: 'If you only knew what God gives' (cf Jn 4:10). They who welcome it can have the experience of a passage to new life (cf. 1 Cor 5:7-8). This passage makes us relish how good God is (cf. 1 Pet 2:1-2), the source of peace and life.

In you is life
Evil
speaks in my heart,
and you, O God,
listen to my groaning.
Your grace
is precious to me.
Quench my thirst
at the stream
of your delights.
In you is life
and all its flowing,
and with you
I hope
to be not mistaken.

CRY OF ANGUISH

from Psalm 69

Save me, O God,
for the waters are closing over me;
I sink into the deepest swamp
where there is no firm ground.
I have come into deep waters,
and the flood overwhelms me.
Exhausted with crying for help,
my throat is parched and my eyes fail,
searching for my God.

May none of those who hope in you
be ashamed through me, O God Most High;
those who seek you must not be disgraced,
because of me, O God of Israel.

I bear reproach for your sake,
and shame has covered my face;
I am cut off from my family,
a stranger to my mother's children.
But I pray to you, O God,
at an acceptable time;
in your great and faithful love,
O God, answer with sure deliverance.

Jesus wanted to touch the depths of human anguish (cf. Mt 26:37-38) and has given us the example of how to get out of it: through unceasing prayer which becomes the search for God's will (cf. Mt 26:39, 42) and total confidence in God's arms (cf. Mt 27:46), the prelude of a certain victory (cf. Acts 2:36). Christians can emerge 'from the deep of the waters', with confidence begin again their exhausting journey, and so win the visible salvation, raising their hearts to Christ.

I am sinking in the mud
O God, I have no more strength to invoke you.
My throat is dry and my heart too.
Bitter solitude is wrapping my soul.
I have become a stranger among my family;
I have become a laughing stock
among the insults of avid friends.
Hear, O good God, our silence,
and your cry becomes the cry of Christ
for a cosmic awakening.

YOU SHALL ANSWER ME

from Psalm 86

Hear me, O God, and answer me,
for I am poor and needy.
Guard me, for I am faithful to you;
save your servant who trusts in you,
for you are my God.

O God, take pity on me,
for I call all day long to you.
Bring joy to your servant,
for I lift up my heart to you.
You are kind and forgiving, O God,
full of faithful love
to all who call to you.

O God, hear my prayer,
and listen to my cry for mercy.
In my day of distress I call to you,
and you will answer me.
Of all the gods, O God,
not one is like you;
no deed can compare with yours.

With all my heart I will sing your praise,
O God, my God;
I will glorify your name forever;
for great is your faithful love for me;
you have saved my soul
from the depths of the grave.

Many times Jesus has emphasised that God the Creator takes care of each of us (cf. Mt 7:7-11), that God the Creator loves us (cf. Jn 16:27), and that God the Creator goes beyond our demands and desires (cf. Lk 11:9-13). God the Creator sent the Son to the world to save it through God (cf. Jn 3:17-18) and in Jesus we have become God's people, heirs, co-heirs (cf. 1 Jn 3:1-2). We are urged to respond, and nothing can separate us from this God-Love (cf. Rom 8:38-39).

Only in this way I will be able to see you
I am a poor person, O God,
and I feel it when I think of you
and your love doesn't embarrass me
though some inquisitive and gossipy looks do.
Your mercy is forgiving kindness.
Who can equal you, O God?
Certainly not human authorities
which do violence
to my desire of growing in freedom.

A MERCIFUL GOD

from Psalm 103

My soul praises you, God,
I praise your holy name
from the depths of my heart.
My soul praises you, God,
I will never forget your kindnesses.

You forgive all my sins,
and cure all my illnesses;
you save my life from the pit,
and crown me with faithful love and mercy;
you satisfy me all my life with goodness,
and renew my youth like an eagle's.

You are just in all you do,
and fair to all the oppressed.
You made your ways known to Moses,
your deeds to the people of Israel.
You are merciful and gracious,
slow to get angry,
full of faithful love.

You will not be always accusing,
nor nurse your anger forever.
You do not act as our sins deserve,
nor give us our due for our offences.
Your faithful love for those who revere you
is as high as the heavens above earth.

The story of God's love for us started with the creation (cf. Gen 1:26) and culminated in Jesus (cf. Jn 3:16), who calls us friends (cf. Jn 15:15), and has given us his Spirit, making us God's people (cf. Rom 8:15). Therefore, every person must bless God, the God of our Lord Jesus Christ, the merciful God of every consolation, the God who helps us in all our troubles (cf. 2 Cor 1:3-4).

O Lord, I would like to bless you always
I would like to say good things about you.
With all my heart I would.
And my faith is still so strong, absolute,
without any doubts
about your unquestionable love.
Doubts? Yes, I have some
but only because I am a human being.
You don't treat us like dust,
and you forgive our sins
with a kindness
which makes me feel
I am your favourite.